Designer Sweatshirts

How to Trim and Alter Sweatshirts

by

Mary Mulari

Handwriting and Illustrations
by the author

Printed in the United States of America

Acknowledgements

for assistance, enthusiasm and ideas:
 Margaret Croswell   Karen Kellogg
 Karen Buell   Jackie Hanson
for their willingness to model sweatshirts on a hot August day :
 my four sisters
 Ruth Koski Benito   Rachel Koski
 Sarah Koski   Rebecca Koski Siiteri
for the supply of sweatshirts and
encouragement :
 Aurora Surplus Store and Barry

ISBN 0-9613569-2-8

Eighth printing - April 1986

Table of Contents

This book is dedicated to

my "Designer Sweatshirt" students
   and their contagious enthusiasm

and to the memory of my grandmothers
      Ida Koski
      Hilja Perämäki
   who had fine taste and skill
   with a needle.

Introducing:
Designer Sweatshirts

The fashion industry has helped the world to develop an appreciation of the sweatshirt. Now that the garment is stylish, more people are realizing its comfort, warmth and durability. Here in northeastern Minnesota, these qualities have long been known; sweatshirts are kept handy year-round for sudden changes in the weather.

Like designer jeans, sweatshirts can become more than plain clothing. With trim and altered necklines, they turn into special garments that are fun to make and wear.

This book will show you how to alter a sweatshirt's basic construction and how to trim. Patterns are included. With the basic information presented, you will be able to design and personalize sweatshirts and other clothing as well.

Read on to begin the journey to fashioning your own "designer sweatshirt"...

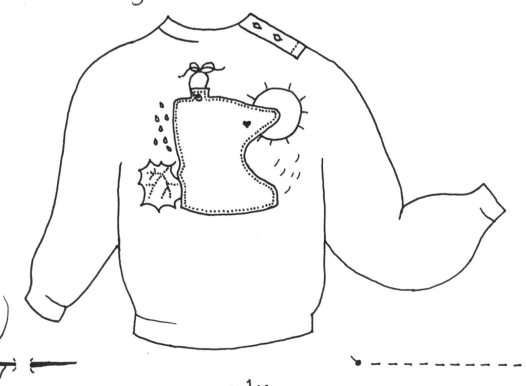

Supplies

Here's what you will need to make your own "designer sweatshirt:"

1. A <u>crew neck sweatshirt</u>. Be sure that it is not old and well-worn. You will be spending a good amount of time working on it so it is wise to begin with a new or nearly new shirt. You will not want your shirt to look washed out when the decorations on it are still bright and fresh.

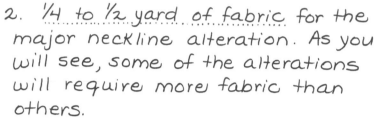

2. <u>¼ to ½ yard of fabric</u> for the major neckline alteration. As you will see, some of the alterations will require more fabric than others.

3. <u>Fabric scraps</u> for decorations. Colorful gingham, small print calico and cotton are popular choices.

4. <u>Thread</u> to match the fabrics you have chosen.

5. Light weight iron-on <u>interfacing</u> to reinforce areas of neckline additions and the back of machine appliqué work. About ½ yard would do.

6. <u>Scissors</u>, <u>pins</u>, ruler and <u>tape measure</u>

7. <u>Paper</u> (such as inexpensive typing paper) to use on the back of machine applique work.

8. An <u>iron</u>. As with all sewing projects, the use of an iron is essential.

9. A <u>seam ripper</u> ... just in case

Do I Need an Expensive Sewing Machine?

To do the sewing and decorating described in this book, you will need a sewing machine that will sew a zigzag stitch. It does not have to be an elaborate new machine with a free arm. The directions and procedures are designed to make the sewing easy and possible for all kinds of sewers and machines.

The best thing you can do is to give your machine a little tender loving care. Remove the dust from the bobbin area, drop in some oil if the manufacturer recommends its use, and keep the machine direction manual handy in case you need to refer to it. If you take the time to read it, you may be surprised at what your machine can do!

NEW TOOLS

From "Designer Sweatshirt" classes I have taught, I have learned that many women are not familiar with sewing tools invented since they were in high school home economics. These tools are time savers for home sewers and useful for many kinds of sewing and craft projects. In case they are new to you, consider adding them to your sewing basket.

The gluestick is literally a stick of glue, similar in size and construction to a tube of lipstick. The glue is white to clear in color. It is a temporary kind of glue for fabrics and is easy to apply. It will not gum up your sewing machine or hand needle and it will wash out of fabrics. It is excellent to use when you want to sew on a narrow piece of trim or rickrack. Rub the gluestick on the back of the trim, pat it into place on the fabric and sew it on. No pins needed!

Stitch Witchery™ is fusible webbing which will permanently attach one fabric to another. It is sold off a bolt (18" wide) and also on rolls ¾" wide. It is white in color and reminds me of compressed spider webs! Both the large flat pieces and the strips off the roll are convenient. You place the Stitch Witchery™ between the two cloth surfaces you wish to attach, then iron on top of the fabric to "melt" the Stitch Witchery™ which welds the fabrics together. Try to keep the surface of your iron away from the fusible webbing — it can make a mess. Follow the instructions that come with the product for more ideas and hints for application.

Washable markers are the answer to the problem of how to mark fabrics so you can see the marks but later get rid of them. These markers look like felt-tip pens with blue pen tips. You can use them to draw fine lines (great for quilters!) which will disappear with water when they are no longer needed. A purple variety of this pen also disappears with water but has the added feature of disappearing on its own in 48 hours. (Someone has named it the "motivation marker.") Once you become accustomed to using these markers, you will wonder how you survived before they were invented. A caution: wet and remove the marks before laundering the garment as detergent can sometimes set the color into the fabric.

Fraycheck™ is a small bottle of clear liquid used on cut edges of fabric to prevent fraying. You will find it useful in preventing seam allowances from raveling.

It seems we never reach the point where we know everything about sewing and sewing products. These are some of the great ones I have found to be useful. Look for them in the notions departments of fabric shops.

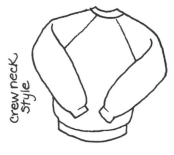

crew neck style

Sweatshirt Colors and Styles

Now that sweatshirts have come out of sweaty gymnasiums and locker rooms, there are more choices in color and style.

Many people select the standard oxford gray sweatshirt for decorating. It is popular because bright calico prints and ginghams look very good as trim on the neutral color background. You might consider choosing a new color. Sweatshirt fleece is being produced in every hue of the color spectrum. You may even decide to sew your own sweatshirt.

A crew-neck sweatshirt is the standard type used for altering and decorating. It is probably the lowest in cost and easiest to find. Manufacturers are branching out in the style department to produce v-necks, hooded sweatshirts, rugby style shirts with collars and plackets already added, multi-color combinations and zipper front jacket styles. These can all be decorated.

Look for more innovative styles in the future. Leisure and action-loving Americans have adopted sweatshirts for year-round wear. Comfortable and soft, sweatshirts are here to stay! They will become even more special with your designer touch.

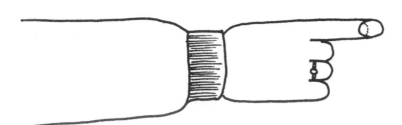

It may seem silly to wash everything before you start, but there are good reasons for laundering your sweatshirt, fabrics, and iron-on interfacing.

Turn the sweatshirt inside out to wash it. This helps to prevent pilling and to preserve the outer fabric surface. If the shirt is a bright color, you may wish to add some white vinegar to cool wash water to "set" the color so it will not run. By washing and drying the shirt before you begin to work on it, you will also set the size so future shrinkage will not occur.

The problems of shrinkage and color running will be eliminated from the decorating fabrics as well by washing and drying them in advance.

Although fusible interfacing is pre-shrunk by the factory, it is a good idea to wash it before use. Soak the interfacing in warm water with a mild soap for 15 minutes. Rinse thoroughly and hang to drip dry. Washing will remove any sizing and save on the wear of your sewing machine needle.

Once everything is dry, you are ready to begin creating your designer sweatshirt.

"Amos says: This space is reserved for notes and sketches of Designer-Sweatshirts-to-be.

How to Shorten a Sweatshirt

Many of the sweatshirts made for adults are actually cut for men's sizing and therefore, some women find the fit to be uncomfortable. The body of the sweatshirt is too long and the ribbing binds tightly around the hips. The sleeves may also be too long.

These problems should be corrected before any other work is done. The first step is to try the shirt on to determine how much to shorten it. Shortening will remove the excess length and bring the binding up to a more comfortable position.

Be cautious about the amount you decide to shorten the shirt and remember to allow for a seam allowance at the bottom. If you cut away too much, you will notice that the sweatshirt is too short in the back.

The basic procedure will be to remove the ribbing, cut away from the body of the sweatshirt and then sew the ribbing back on at the new bottom edge.

1. Measure up from the top of the ribbing to the amount you wish to remove from the shirt. Mark this amount at frequent intervals around the shirt.

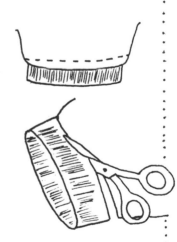

2. Insert scissors into seam attaching ribbing to sweatshirt body and carefully cut the ribbing off the sweatshirt. Set aside. Then cut around the sweatshirt at your marks to remove the excess length.

3. Place a pin to mark each quarter portion on both ribbing and new sweatshirt bottom. Re-attach the binding to the sweatshirt body by matching the pins and adjusting the fabric between. The right side of the binding will face the right side of the sweatshirt.

4. Sew this seam with a stretch stitch (elastic overlock) if your machine has one. This will allow the new seam to give when stretched. If you cannot use a stretch stitch,

use a small zigzag stitch and pull slightly on the fabrics as you sew. Turn the ribbing back down.

    5. Sleeves can also be shortened with this method.

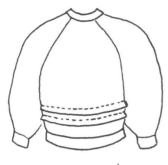

Another method of shortening is to sew tucks around the body of the sweatshirt. You will need to determine the amount of excess length in order to determine the size of the tucks. Remember that a tuck sewn into the shirt reduces its length by twice the depth of the tuck. For example, a ½" wide tuck actually takes up 1" of length.

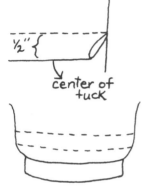

center of tuck

    1. Measure up from the top of the ribbing to the distance where you wish to locate the center of your first tuck. Mark this amount at frequent intervals around the shirt. If you plan to sew in more than one tuck, mark their center lines also.

    2. Turn the bottom of the sweatshirt up and inside until you form the fold on the lowest tuck centerline. Pin this fold securely all the way around the shirt. Sew around the shirt, using the seam gauge on the machine to guide you. For example, use the ½" mark as a guide if you want a ½" tuck.

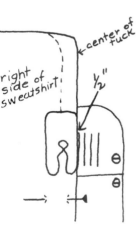

center of tuck

right side of sweatshirt

½"

    3. Turn the sweatshirt up to form the folds for other tucks. Pin and sew in the same manner.

    4. Iron the tucks down toward the bottom of the shirt.

PLACKETS

A placket is an attractive and comfortable alteration to the neckline of a sweatshirt. It can be placed center front, on the raglan sleeve seam, or on the shoulder. The procedure for sewing will be the same for each location.

First determine the length of your finished placket and add at least 2 inches. See the pattern for the placket at the back of the book. Note that one long edge will be placed on the fold.

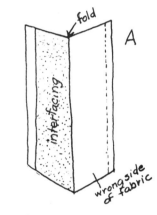

1. Cut 2 placket pieces from fabric. Cut a piece of fusible interfacing for half of each placket, as shown on diagram A. One edge will be against the foldline and the other edge will be ½" away from the cut edge of the fabric to allow for the seam allowance. Apply interfacing to each placket piece in this way. Turn in the seam allowances on both long edges of both pieces and iron. (Diagram B). This will indicate the actual, finished width of the placket. Then turn the seam allowances back out.

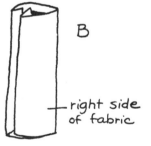

2. Mark the exact center line of chosen placket location on sweatshirt front. Draw this line with washable marker from neck edge to bottom edge of placket location.

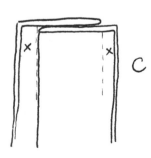

3. Place one placket piece on top of the other, lining up the interfaced areas and leaving seam allowances extended. (I prefer to use the interfaced sides of the placket pieces as the back sides of the placket. To arrange this, place interfaced halves on top, as indicated by the "x's" on diagram C.)

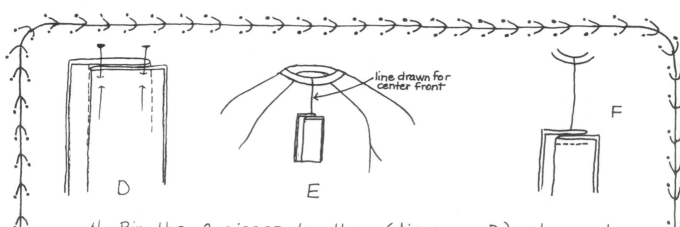

D   E   F

line drawn for center front

4. Pin the 2 pieces together (diagram D), place at bottom of placket location and pin to sweatshirt. The top placket piece will have the fold to the left, seam allowances to the right. This will be correct alignment for a woman's placket opening. At this point, placket pieces will hang down toward bottom of shirt. (Diagram E).

5. Sew a straight seam across the pieces at the location of the bottom of the placket location. Sew only through the interfaced areas and the sweatshirt and leaving seam allowances free of stitching. See diagram F.

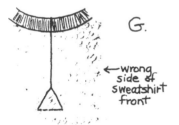

G.

← wrong side of sweatshirt front

6. Cut down from neck edge on marked line. Stop about one inch above stitched line and cut diagonally to ends of seam. Wrong side of sweatshirt will look like diagram G.

7. Turn placket pieces up toward neck edge. Tuck seam allowances back inside as you originally ironed them. Tuck sweatshirt cut edge inside placket piece. You will need to work with the bottom corners to get a smooth look. Pin each side into place. There should be extra fabric extending past the neck ribbing. Cut away the excess but leave ¼" – ½" to turn inside the placket to form the top edge. Sew both sides from the bottom to the top and across.

sweatshirt front

8. To secure the placket, sew a rectangle at the bottom through both left and right sides. Add buttons and buttonholes, snaps, or leave the opening plain.

Use this placket method in any garment. It is easy and the end result is neat.

Collar with Front Facing Panels

This neckline alteration is a pleasing addition to a crewneck sweatshirt. It consists of two facings, one showing in the front as a decorative yoke and the other lining the back of the opening, and a collar sewn to the top edge of the ribbing.

Find the collar and facing patterns in the pattern section. Cut 2 facing pieces from fabric and mark the stitching lines on the wrong side of one facing piece.

1. Mark the center front line on the front of the sweatshirt. Place the two facing pieces with right sides together at the top of the neck edge and centered on the line you drew. Stitch the seam as indicated on the wrong side of the facing, sewing one stitch across the point of the "v." Cut from neckline edge to point, cutting through sweatshirt and two facings. Turn top facing to back of shirt. Press opening. Turn back the edges of both top and back facings about ½" and press. Pin into place and machine stitch from the top, catching both top and bottom facing in the stitching line.

2. Measure around neckline ribbing, trying not to pull or distort the ribbing. Add one inch to the measurement for seam allowances and cut the two collars to that length. Fuse interfacing to one collar. Sew the 2 collars together using ½" seam allowance. (see diagram below). Trim seam and turn collar right side out.

½" {   } ½"

Leave top ½" free of stitching on each side of the collar.

3. Pin neck edge of right side of collar to the wrong side of the neck ribbing. (I prefer to use the collar side _not_ interfaced as the right side.) Do not stretch neck edge. Collar will fit if you measured correctly. Sew a ½" seam. (See diagram.) Turn back ½" on the other raw collar edge and hand sew into place on right side of neck edge. You can then topstitch around the collar and the "v" opening.

The collar will open up the neckline edge and spread the facings open so there is a wider neck opening. If you do not want this to happen, place a loop and button or ties directly below the collar.

Variations and additions to consider:

♥ lace or trim added to collar and outer edges of front facing (use gluestick to apply the trim)

♥ sew tucks into fabric before you cut the front facing piece

♥ Use only one facing and turn it to the inside of the sweatshirt

♥ You can probably go on to devise some great ideas of your own!

Children ♥ Designer Sweatshirts

CARDIGAN

This is a variation that can be worn by all ages, from young toddlers to grandmas who find it difficult to pull a crewneck sweatshirt over their heads. It also serves well as a lightweight jacket.

1. Find and mark the center front of the sweatshirt. Use a yardstick to draw a straight, dark line from the neck ribbing to the bottom of the shirt.

2. Measure the length of the line and add at least 2 inches. Extend the placket pattern to this length and cut 2 long plackets. These two strips will form the button and buttonhole sides of the cardigan front. As you did with the placket pieces, interface one side of each strip, from the fold out to the edge of the seam allowance.

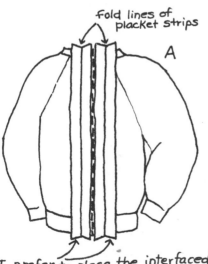

Fold lines of placket strips

A

I prefer to place the interfaced halves of the placket strips on the sides.

dashed line indicates center front line

placket strips will extend 1" beyond top and bottom of shirt

3. Now you are ready to sew the strips to the sweatshirt. Place one long edge of each strip, right side down, on each side of the center front line (see diagram A). Pin them in place. Sew each strip to the sweatshirt using a ½" seam allowance from the center line. Stitch from the bottom of the sweatshirt to the top. Then cut the sweatshirt open on the line you drew.

wrong side of sweatshirt

B

4. Turn the long free edge of each fabric strip to the back of the shirt. Iron back a ½" seam allowance on the long edge and pin the edge into place over the line of machine stitching. (See diagram B.) Turn under the excess fabric at the top and bottom to form finished ends even with the ribbing. Pin into place.

5. Topstitch around each placket strip on the right side of the sweatshirt. This will insure a neat, even seamline visible from the front when the sweatshirt is worn.

Add buttonholes and buttons, snaps, ties or velcro dots.

Sketch your Designer Sweatshirt here ↓

:NOTES:·

try a collar round
make a square collar
like a sailor collar
extending around front
You might have to
cut some azul neck
ribbing off
use lettuce edging
around y alk

Jackie's Lettuce Edge Neckline and Cuffs

A special feminine touch can be added to the ribbing of a sweatshirt neckline and sleeve cuffs. At first glance, this ruffly look will seem to be trim added to the shirt, but it is not.

Select a thread color to contrast with the color of the sweatshirt. Use it for both top and bobbin threads. Adjust your sewing machine to the appliqué or buttonhole stitch. Place the outside edge of the ribbing under

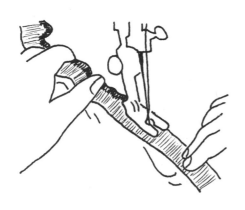

the presser foot and begin stitching. You will need to stretch the ribbing behind and ahead of your work, as shown in the diagram. Do not hesitate – pull firmly. This distorting of the ribbing and the stitching which holds the distortion in place creates the "lettuce" edge of ruffles.

For a solid look to your stitching, sew around twice, pulling the second time around also.

This trim is simple to do and fun. It is eye-catching and disguises the plain look of a sweat-shirt. You can also consider adding it to necklines with placket openings.

Shirt Tail Bottom

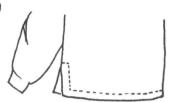

Sometime you may wish to create a different look at the bottom of your sweatshirt. Many women find the shirt tail style to be comfortable as it allows more room for the hips.

1. Find the shirt tail pattern and cut 2 from fabric. (Fabric used will not be highly visible, but should complement the sweatshirt color.) Mark the stitching lines on the wrong sides of the fabric. Turn back once and stitch the sides and top of each facing.

2. Cut bottom ribbing off sweatshirt. Find and mark with a line the exact sides of the shirt.

3. Pin right side of facing to right side of shirt at center of shirt side. Sew on stitching lines, with one stitch across the point of the "v." Cut to the point, turn facing to inside of shirt and press. Secure facings in place by hand sewing, fusible webbing or top stitching by machine.

4. Cut 2 strips of the same fabric used for shirt tails. The strips would be at least one inch wide and 2 inches longer than the new bottom edges of your sweatshirt. Pin one long edge in place on the shirt with right side of fabric to right side of shirt. There will be one-inch extending on each end.

Sew into place across bottom of shirt. Turn facing to back of shirt and press. Turn under about ½" on the top edge of the facing and press.

Turn in the excess fabric on the ends. Attach facing to shirt with fusible webbing, hand sewing or top-stitching.

More ideas: Repeat facing fabric in a design on the shirt.
• Allow some of bottom edge fabric to show on right side of shirt
• Use 2 shirt tail facings, one on the inside and one on the outside of the shirt on each side.

  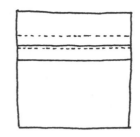

Sleeve Pocket

Pocket patterns can be found in the pattern section of this book. These pockets are designed for use on the sleeves of sweatshirts but they could be placed elsewhere also.

1. Turn back and press the sides and bottom edges of the pocket. Fold back the top on the foldline indicated on the pattern. Trim can be added.

2. Measure down the sleeve from the neck ribbing. Place the top edge of the pocket 9-10 inches down from the neck edge and in the middle of the sleeve. (For small children, pocket would be higher - about 7-8 inches down from the neck edge.) The correct location is the center of the upper arm.

3. Pin the pocket in place, using many pins to hold it securely. There will be enough room in the sleeve to sew the pocket by machine even if you do not have a free arm model.

Additional ways to trim pockets: lace, buttons, a flap over the top, tucks. For a child, a "surprise" inside the pocket is fun. This could be a small stuffed doll, a piece of candy, a toy. Let your imagination bring you other ideas!

machine appliqué

The dictionary tells us that appliqué is the process of sewing or fixing one piece of material ornamentally to another piece of material. Machine appliqué is a technique and skill which develops with practice and with learning how one's sewing machine operates to produce an even stitch. Each sewing machine adjusts and operates differently so you will need to refer to your machine operation manual.

The machine appliqué stitch is basically a zigzag stitch (ʌʌʌ) jammed close together (ʍʍʍ) so that it looks more solid and is also stronger. It would be similar to, but wider than, the side of a buttonhole. An estimate of a good width would be between 1/16" and 1/8".

Practice before beginning on your sweatshirt...

Use a medium size machine needle (size 14 or European 90). Use 100% cotton or poly-cotton thread of good quality. If you have an embroidery presser foot, attach it to your machine. There is a groove cut into the bottom which allows built-up stitching to pass under more easily. Loosen the top tension on your machine. (Check your machine manual if you do not know how to do this.) This will force the top thread to go through the fabric and catch the bobbin thread below, creating a smooth look to your top stitches. This will also eliminate the need to change bobbin thread colors; the bobbin thread will not be seen from the top of the fabric.

Experiment with your machine to find the settings where you best like the look of the appliqué stitch. Take note of the settings and record them in your machine manual or directly on the machine.

Practice sewing around curves, corners and points. Stitching should be at the edge of and completely on the fabric you are appliquéing to the background.

Now you are ready to begin machine appliqué stitching on your designer sweatshirt.

1. First you must select a design; a few are included in this book. Trace the design onto white paper for a working copy that can be cut apart.

2. Iron a piece of fusible interfacing onto the back of the fabric you plan to use. Cut the design out of the interfaced fabric. (Interfacing is needed to give strength and stability to fabric.) Remember to reverse the design if it has different right and left sides. Add an extension to any pieces placed under others.

3. Use fusible webbing, gluestick or pins to attach design pieces to sweatshirt. You will want to attach the pieces firmly. On the back of the sweatshirt fabric and underneath the design area, pin a piece of paper larger than the design. One pin in each corner is adequate. The paper will help your machine to sew more evenly and eliminate the "wavy" effect which occurs when sewing on knit fabrics. Stitch 'N Tear Pellon® can be used in place of paper.

4. Decide on the order of sewing. If there are overlapping pieces, plan which ones to sew first.

5. Use matching or contrasting thread. If you are a beginner in machine appliqué, you may want to use matching thread so the stitching will not be as obvious.

6. As you stitch, manuever the fabric without pulling or spreading it. You will not be getting anywhere fast as you sew; stitching back and forth close together does not produce rapid progress. Practice patience with this kind of sewing!

7. When you finish, pull the top threads to the sweatshirt back and tie knots. Tear away and discard the paper or Stitch 'N Tear Pellon®.

8. Iron the design on the back and front.

Appliqué by Hand Sewing

Often when I suggest hand stitching to apply appliqué designs, many women will groan and let me know they will do anything to escape sewing by hand! I remind them that hand appliqué work does have some advantages: it can be done when one does not have access to a sewing machine and it probably takes no more time than machine appliqué stitching. Remember - it takes a long time to guide the sewing machine needle around a shape while machine appliquéing.

In case I have gained your interest to try hand appliqué, here is what you will need to do:

1. Add ¼" seam allowances to all design pieces. This is the amount of fabric you will turn under as you stitch. Cut the original shape out of fusible interfacing and iron it onto the fabric, leaving seam allowances free of interfacing.

2. Pin or gluestick design shapes in place on the sweatshirt, keeping seam allowances free. You do not need to add paper to the back of the sweatshirt fabric as you do with machine appliqué.

3. Thread a hand sewing needle with thread that matches the fabric. Turn under seam allowances as you stitch. Clip into seam allowance when necessary to form a smooth shape. Use small stitches for a firm and hidden attachment.

Add fancy embroidery stitches to embellish your work, if you wish.

Design Placement

Here are some things to think about while deciding "what to place where" to decorate a sweatshirt.

1. Try to balance your design shapes. Avoid placing everything on one side of the shirt. A small design on the upper left front of a shirt which has a center placket could be offset by a larger design on the lower right front. A placket on the shoulder or raglan seam will allow room to center a design on the shirt front.

2. Don't forget the back of the sweatshirt! We do not see it when we wear the shirt, but others do. Repeat a part of your design on the back to add interest.

3. Sleeves and shoulders can be trimmed. Take care not to place a design at the narrow end of a sleeve because your sewing machine will not operate well in such "tight quarters." (How about hand stitching?) ☺

4. For women, avoid placing large prominent designs over the area of the breasts. This area would be approximately in line with the "armpits" of the shirt.

5. Consider placing designs around the neckline area to imitate the "Fair Isle" sweater yoke pattern.

6. Monograms are popular. A small monogram could be placed on the upper left side of the shirt. Use 2-3" letters and overlap them. A monogram could also be appliquéd to the upper sleeve in place of a pocket.

Think about adding a pair of sweatpants to your sweatshirt for a "designer sweatsuit"! A small design or part of a design from the sweatshirt could be repeated on the knee or lower leg. Avoid trimming any areas of the lower body which you do not want to emphasize! ☺

Where to Find Appliqué Patterns and Ideas

Have you ever thought of adding an appliqué to a garment and then given up the idea because you had no patterns or ideas? It will help you to start a collection of patterns ... but where will you find them?

The most common suggestion is children's coloring books. This idea is only partially good because most coloring books have pictures with too many details. The best coloring books for appliqué designs are the simple ABC books for very young children.

If you like full-size designs, check the handcraft books in your library. Books on making your own greeting cards and those offering stitching patterns for quilting will often contain some unique ideas to transfer to appliqué. Several craft and needlework magazines also feature full-size designs. Designs on small grids are usable if you are willing to transfer them to a larger scale.

Look around you for ideas. Check your paper towels and paper napkins for fruit and kitchen shapes. Trace a cute pattern from a decorated purchased shirt. Try drawing on your own — simple designs work best and great detail is not needed. Share patterns with friends. Look for clever ideas in the gift catalogs you get in the mail.

Once you start to accumulate a design collection, keep everything together in an envelope or folder. Instead of cutting up your original patterns, re-trace a design on other paper to make a working copy, thereby leaving your pattern collection neat and complete.

* A new resource for appliqué patterns is my second book, <u>Appliqué Design Collection</u>. See page 40.

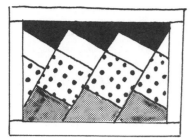

Seminole Patchwork

An intricate-looking but easy technique for decorating clothing was developed by the Seminole Indians in Florida. Its popularity is growing and it is certainly an interesting way to decorate sweatshirts and other clothing.

You begin by cutting strips of fabric. Plain colored fabrics are traditional and effective; small prints work well also, but should be chosen carefully. The strips should all be the same length but you can vary the widths for an interesting look. As an example, you could cut 4 strips, one 2" wide, one 1" wide, one 1½" wide and one 3" wide. (Plan that ½" in each strip will be taken up in seam allowances.)

Sew together the strips you have cut. Use ¼" seam allowances and stitch with right sides of fabrics together. You will create a wide band of "striped" fabric. Iron the seam allowances toward the bottom of the strip.

Cut the band into pieces of equal size.

Sew these small pieces together, offsetting each segment, as shown in the diagram. Press the seam allowances in one direction. You may wish to fuse interfacing to the back as a stabilizer.

Turn back the edges to form straight sides on the band of patchwork. Another strip of one of the fabrics used in the patchwork can be sewn to each side, as shown at the top of the page. This will "frame" the patchwork and stabilize the bias piecing. Sew Seminole patchwork pieces to sweatshirt by hand or machine. For many other ways to assemble and use Seminole patchwork, read The Seminole Patchwork Book by Cheryl Greider Bradkin, a Yours Truly Publication.

Double Needles

It is a great pleasure to introduce sewers to an item that has been hiding in the sewing machine accessory box for years. A common response to the question "Have you ever used a double needle?" is "No, I got one with my sewing machine but I've never used it."

To use a double needle, you need to have a zigzag sewing machine. Double needles can be purchased at most fabric shops in case you did not get one with your machine. You do not need two bobbins; the bobbin thread services both needles as you sew.

You will need two sources of thread at the top of your machine. Thread each one through the machine and into one needle. You may want to loosen the top tension slightly.

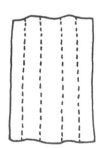

The double needles form a slight tuck in the fabric as you sew. The stitching will be more obvious if you use a contrasting thread color. To stitch a straight line, use a yardstick and a washable marker to draw on the sweatshirt. Then stitch with the line between the 2 needles.

Have fun with double needles! Try them on other clothing too. They add a look of "high quality."

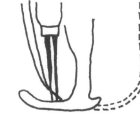

Waste Canvas

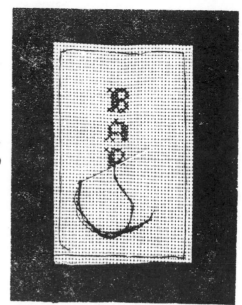

If you have wanted a good way to embroider on plain fabric with good markings to guide you and without the mess of iron-on designs, waste canvas is what you have been looking for. Using it will allow you to neatly cross-stitch a design onto your sweatshirt.

Waste canvas looks and feels like thin needlepoint canvas. It is very stiff and consists of threads woven together with "holes" in between where the needle goes in and out.

You will need a charted design for this work— counted cross stitch, knitting and needlepoint designs can be used. Count the number of squares horizontally and vertically in the design. Count the holes in the canvas in the same way and then cut a piece of canvas larger than the design. (Add at least one inch in each direction.) Baste the canvas onto the sweatshirt, sewing around the edges by hand or machine.

Follow the design and cross stitch over the canvas threads and through the sweatshirt fabric. Knot threads in the back of the sweatshirt fabric.

When embroidery is completed, remove the basting stitches. Wet the canvas and you will find it becomes limp. Pull the canvas threads out and discard them. Tweezers help to remove threads in areas of heavy stitching. Be careful— pull slowly.

Waste canvas comes in various sizes. Size numbers refer to number of x-stitches per inch. I recommend sizes 14, 16, and 18 because the embroidery looks very "solid" and individual "x's" are not obvious. You would use 2 strands of floss for size 18 and 3 strands for sizes 14 and 16. Cut the strands about 12" long — longer threads get frayed and worn before they are worked into the design. Good quality, colorfast embroidery floss, such as DMC, is recommended.

Happy stitching — you will be pleased with the results!

Stenciling

Many old techniques of handwork and decoration are being revived. Stenciling is one of them. Decorating magazines show the use of stenciling in the home and on room accessories. Stenciling can be done on fabric with special paints that survive the washing machine. New fabric dyes have been developed which are heat-set with an iron. You might practice on other fabric before you begin your sweatshirt. Slight mistakes or imperfections add to the "charm" of the stenciling work!

Many good instructions and supplies are available to learn this craft.

You could fashion your own "ski sweater" sweatshirt by repeating several designs across the upper front and back of a sweatshirt.

The possibilities are endless · · ·

Other Ways to Trim

Besides cotton calico, there are many other fabrics and trims to select for decorations on a sweatshirt.

Any fabric that is <u>washable</u> could be used. Some suggestions: velour, fake fur, double and single knits, even Ultrasuede! Dig through your supply of fabric scraps for more ideas.

Eyes on animals are a small detail difficult to appliqué... consider using buttons instead.

Rickrack, eyelet lace, ribbon, and woven trims add interesting details. A strip of blue rickrack below a whale would represent water. (This would be a good opportunity to use up the scraps of trim you have not thrown away.)

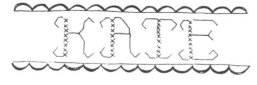

Ribband™ is a product that has been used by counted cross-stitchers and is excellent trim for sweatshirts. It looks like a band of counted thread fabric with lacy edging. A simple cross-stitch design can be embroidered repeatedly across a strip. A child's name could be embroidered for a personal touch. Hand sew the completed Ribband™ onto the sweatshirt.

Perhaps you would like to design a little girl's face to trim a shirt. To make short curly hair, wind washable yarn closely around a strip of paper 1½" wide and 8" long. Sew by machine down the middle and then tear the paper away. Twist & turn the yarn loops and you will have curly hair to sew around a face.

A piece of quilt batting or fleece under an appliquéd shape will pad a design, giving the look of trapunto. Make sure the stuffing you use is washable.

Once you get started on this creative process, you will find many more ideas. I hope these suggestions have stirred up your imagination.

Designing Sweatshirts for Others

You may have a special friend or relative who would love to have a Designer Sweatshirt but you don't know how to decide what to put on the shirt.

With pen in hand, consider the person and what you know about her. Make a list of her favorite colors, hobbies, collections, her job, special aspects of her personality. Writing these things often helps to focus on some good ideas. A quilter friend would be happy to receive a sweatshirt decorated with a quilt square. Hand quilting it to the sweatshirt would be a nice extra touch. Does your cousin collect angels or have a kitchen decorated with mushrooms? Use one of these for a sweatshirt theme.

Do you and a friend have a long-standing joke or a favorite expression? Maybe you could invent a tasteful way to include it on a shirt. Does someone you know always forget your phone number? Embroider the number toward the bottom of the sleeve where she can easily read it.

You may be tempted to create a sweatshirt for a joke for someone's milestone birthday. You will soon realize that too much work and cost go into a sweatshirt for it to become a "worn-only-one-time" garment. You could add "Sporty 40" in an inconspicuous way or on a removable pocket. (A sweat-shirt with "40" emblazoned across the chest may not be worn again once the birthday party is over!)

A monogram always adds a personal touch. Use all 3 initials, first and last only, or just the first initial. It could be part of a design, such as on the sail of a sail-boat. Use waste canvas to apply a small monogram above the sleeve cuff or on the upper sleeve.

Above all, try to be considerate of the receiver of the sweatshirt. Let what you know about the person guide you in making selections of color and trim. Your creative ideas can produce a sweatshirt that will be a very precious gift to a special person.

Ideas for Men and Boys

It seems as if there are many clever ideas for sweatshirts for females, but ideas for men and boys are limited. Many men and boys would not wear a sweatshirt trimmed with a colorful placket and bunches of hearts, balloons or bunnies. It is senseless, then, to spend the time sewing something splashy if the recipient will not wear the finished product. Boys, even at a young age, are particular, so ask questions before you begin. A boy's "favorite thing" (hockey stick and puck, cowboy boots, bicycle, etc.) would be a safe choice. Collars and plackets could be eliminated and the neckline could be left plain. Consider using plaid fabrics as trim for a masculine look.

For men, I have developed more subtle trims. With the double needle, I sewed three stripes across the chest. In addition, I used waste canvas to add a small monogram above the stripes. A darker, contrasting thread was used for both. These trims did not take a great deal of time, but they added an interesting, personalized look to a plain v-neck sweatshirt.

For a sportsman you could use waste canvas to embroider a duck, a wild animal or a small outdoor scene. For a man who enjoys boating or sailing, use the marine flags to spell his name or a boat's name. The flags are fairly simple to duplicate and can be found in encyclopedias in the "flag" section.

It will help you to know the taste and personalities of the males for whom you want to create a sweatshirt.

By the time you have read through to this page, I hope you are feeling inspired to begin a designer sweat-shirt. The process is a creative one and can lead you in the direction of trimming other kinds of clothing also. Many of us who sew appreciate the idea of creating clothing that looks unique, even if only in a small detail.

It has been a great pleasure for me to teach "designer sweatshirt" classes and now to share this information with you through a book. I believe that you will enjoy your attempts to create special sweatshirts and experience the satisfaction that comes from producing a unique garment.

Good luck to you! I think you will have fun with this project. And when you're done, don't forget to sew in the tag that says, "An Original By _____." ← You. We really ought to sign our works of art!

Mary

Miscellaneous Sketches and Ideas

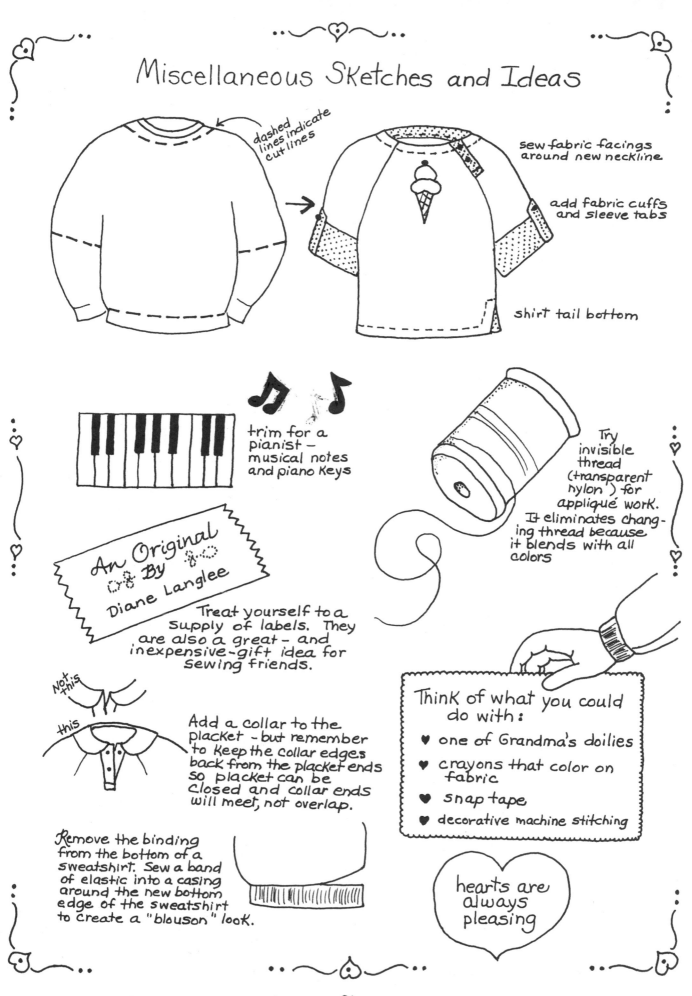

dashed lines indicate cut lines

sew fabric facings around new neckline

add fabric cuffs and sleeve tabs

shirt tail bottom

trim for a pianist — musical notes and piano keys

Try invisible thread (transparent nylon) for appliqué work. It eliminates changing thread because it blends with all colors

An Original By Diane Langlee

Treat yourself to a supply of labels. They are also a great - and inexpensive - gift idea for sewing friends.

Not this

this

Add a collar to the placket - but remember to keep the collar edges back from the placket ends so placket can be closed and collar ends will meet, not overlap.

Think of what you could do with:
- ♥ one of Grandma's doilies
- ♥ crayons that color on fabric
- ♥ snap tape
- ♥ decorative machine stitching

Remove the binding from the bottom of a sweatshirt. Sew a band of elastic into a casing around the new bottom edge of the sweatshirt to create a "blouson" look.

hearts are always pleasing

Appliqué Patterns

P.S. Keep your
book whole...
trace these
patterns on other
paper when you
want to use them.

Nancy's
Raspberry
Jam

whale

crayon

Alteration Patterns*

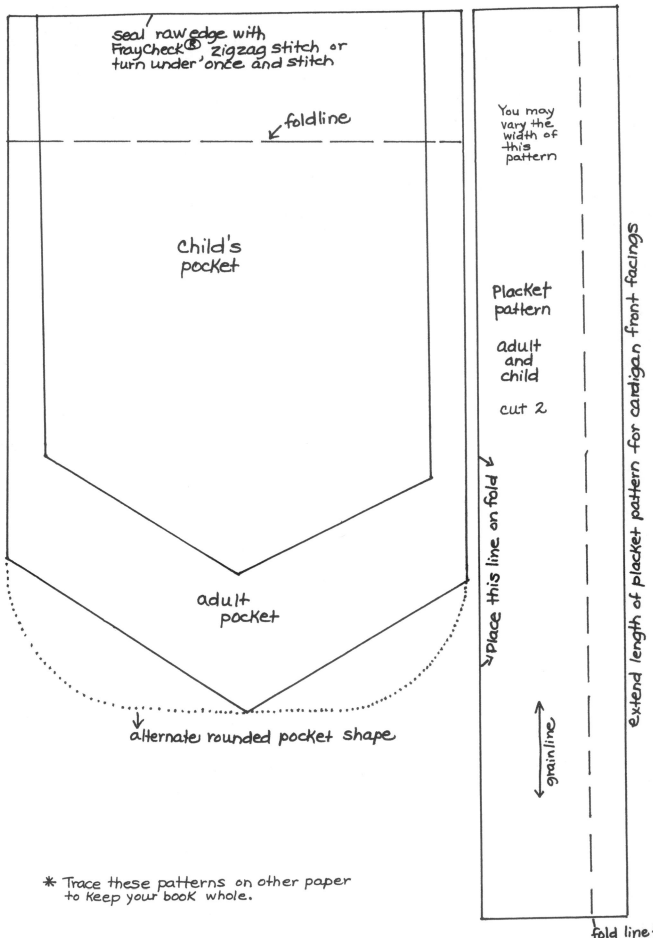

seal raw edge with FrayCheck® zigzag stitch or turn under once and stitch

↙ foldline

Child's pocket

adult pocket

↓ alternate rounded pocket shape

You may vary the width of this pattern

Placket pattern

adult and child

cut 2

↙ Place this line on fold ↙

extend length of placket pattern for cardigan front facings

↕ grainline

fold line for seam allowance

* Trace these patterns on other paper to keep your book whole.

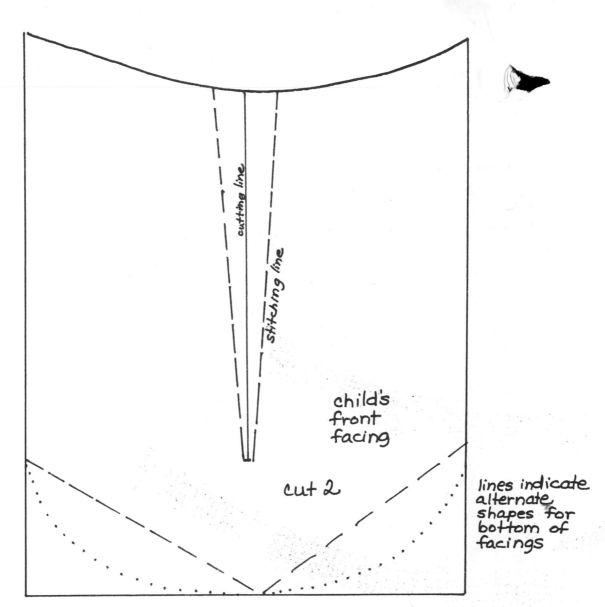

cutting line

stitching line

child's
front
facing

cut 2

lines indicate
alternate
shapes for
bottom of
facings

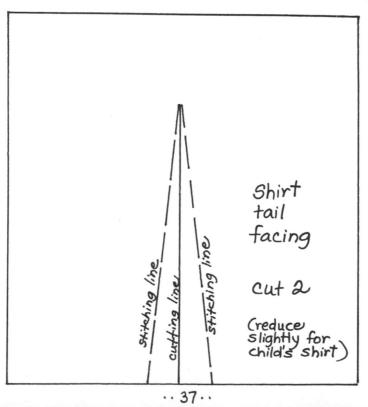

stitching line

cutting line

stitching line

Shirt
tail
facing

cut 2

(reduce
slightly for
child's shirt)

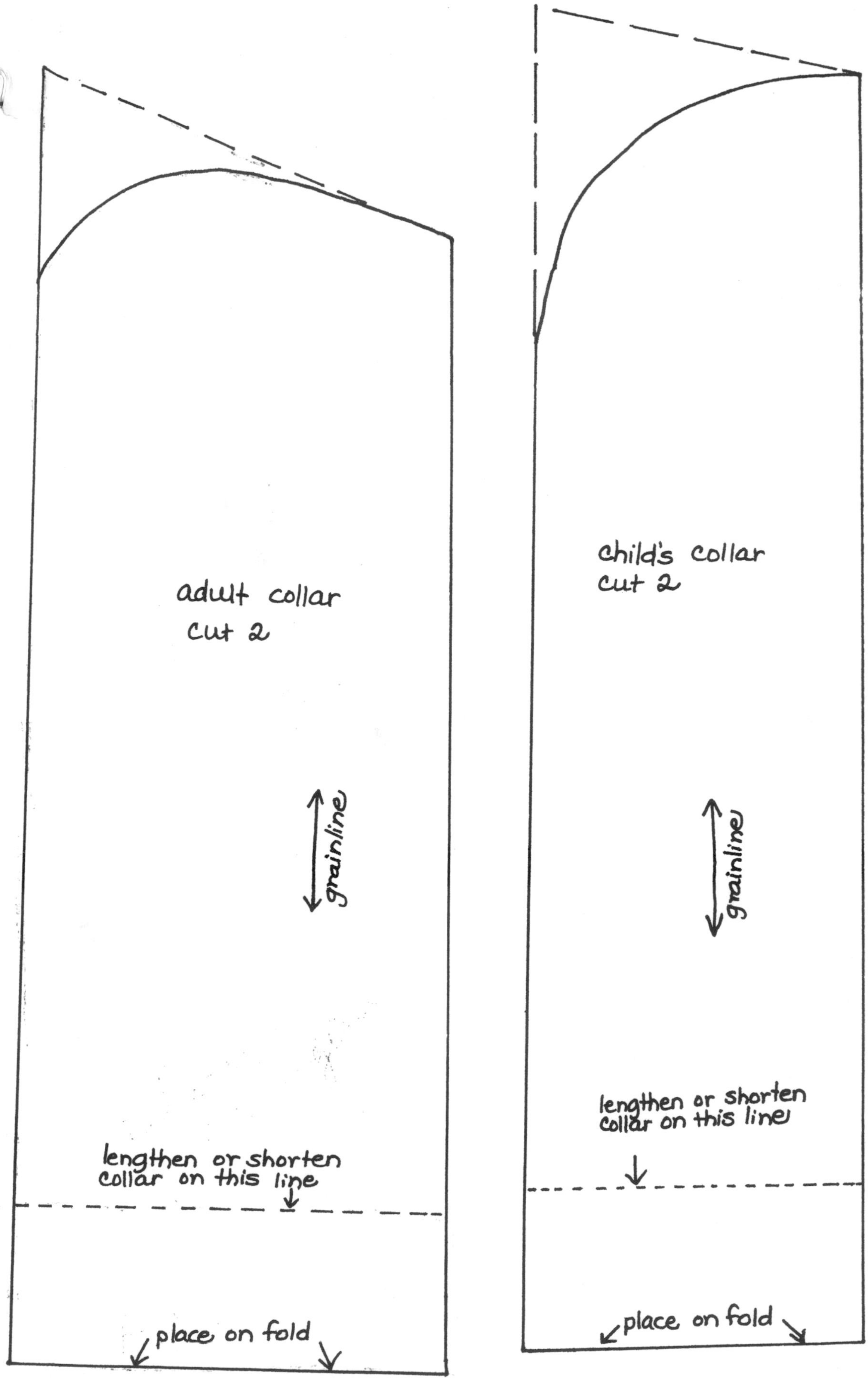

adult collar
cut 2

grainline

lengthen or shorten
collar on this line

place on fold

child's collar
cut 2

grainline

lengthen or shorten
collar on this line

place on fold

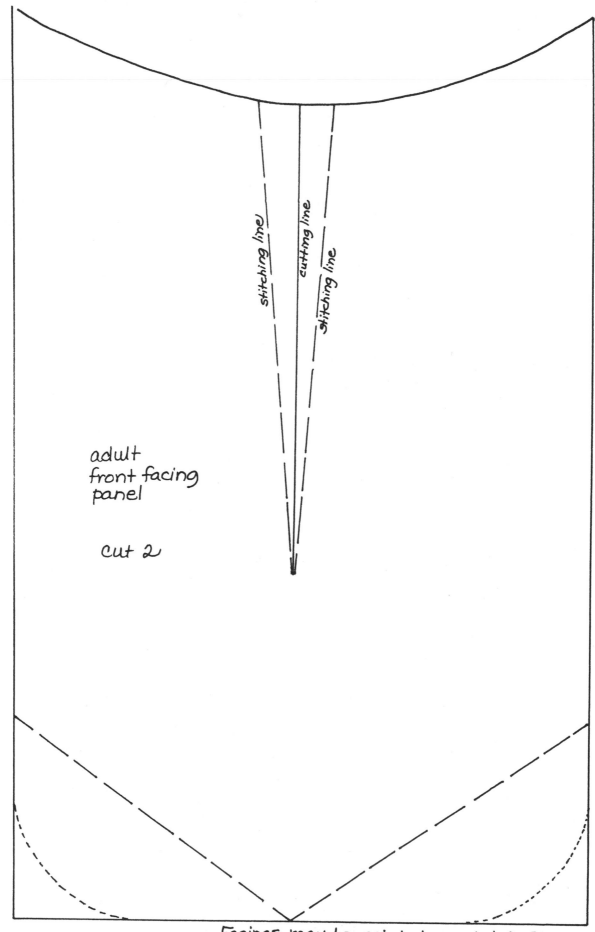

adult
front facing
panel

cut 2

stitching line

cutting line

stitching line

Facings may be pointed, rounded or square at the bottom edge.

A few words about the author:

(This is the "human interest" section of the book and you can skip it if you're in a hurry to begin a designer sweatshirt of your own!)

My interest in sewing began during childhood when I learned to use a treadle sewing machine and when I learned to sew as a member of the Loon Lake 4-H Club. More recently I have been a junior high school English teacher, a store owner-clerk-advertising writer and a student in needle-work classes.

This book was written in response to continued interest in decorating sweatshirts and the "Designer Sweatshirt" classes and seminars I teach.

For additional copies of this book or Applique Design Collection (my book of applique patterns) or for more information, please write to me:

Mary Mulari
Box 87 Dept. B
Aurora, Minnesota 55705